PORTLAND

PORTLAND

JONATHAN NICHOLAS
TEXT AND CAPTIONS

C. BRUCE FORSTER
PHOTOGRAPHY

ADDITIONAL PHOTOGRAPHS BY
RICK SCHAFER

GRAPHIC ARTS CENTER PUBLISHING COMPANY, PORTLAND, OREGON

International Standard Book Number 1-55868-039-X
Library of Congress Catalog Number 90-71081
© MCMXC by Graphic Arts Center Publishing Company
P.O. Box 10306 • Portland, Oregon 97210 • 503/226-2402
Editor-in-Chief • Douglas A. Pfeiffer
Managing Editor • Jean Andrews
Photos by Rick Schafer • Pages 19, 20, 23, 112, lower back jacket
Designer • Robert Reynolds
Typographer • Harrison Typesetting, Inc.
Color Separator • Wy'east Color, Inc.
Printer • Graphic Arts Center, Inc.
Text Paper • Barber-Ellis Fine Paper
Basis 100, LithoFect Plus Gloss • Manufactured by Repap
Bindery • Lincoln & Allen
Printed in the United States of America

To the good citizens of Portland,
the riches of the city.
JONATHAN NICHOLAS

Lots of sizzle; no steak. Pretty wrapping; no presence inside. The thing Portlanders like best about the Portland Building is the statue that sits on the pedestal above its front door. ◄◄ Portland may be a place where citizens prize modesty above all virtues. But it is not free of developers who give new buildings self-important names. This glass dome sits under a tower dubbed *One Financial Center.* Its tenants include real estate brokers and lawyers, but not a single financial centrist. ►

Portlanders give nicknames to buildings they like. In 1983, when the sun first rose on the forty-three-story U.S. Bancorp Tower, citizens promptly named the structure *Big Pink*. The Hilton Hotel, on the other hand, has never been called anything but *The Hilton Hotel*. ◄ Pioneer Courthouse, surrounded by new buildings, remains the pretty face standing out in a crowd. ▲ Dawn finds a mirror waiting on the westside waterfront. ►►

Portlanders enjoy searching for fresh insights, seeking out new perspectives. Facilitating this fondness, the mirrored glass skin of Security Pacific Plaza casts a fractured glance toward its neighbors. ▲ Some cities rush to tear down the old to throw up the new. Portland is more careful. It works hard to save what it likes best about its past. This juxtaposition of form and style, of color and texture, is the hallmark of downtown's architecture. ▶

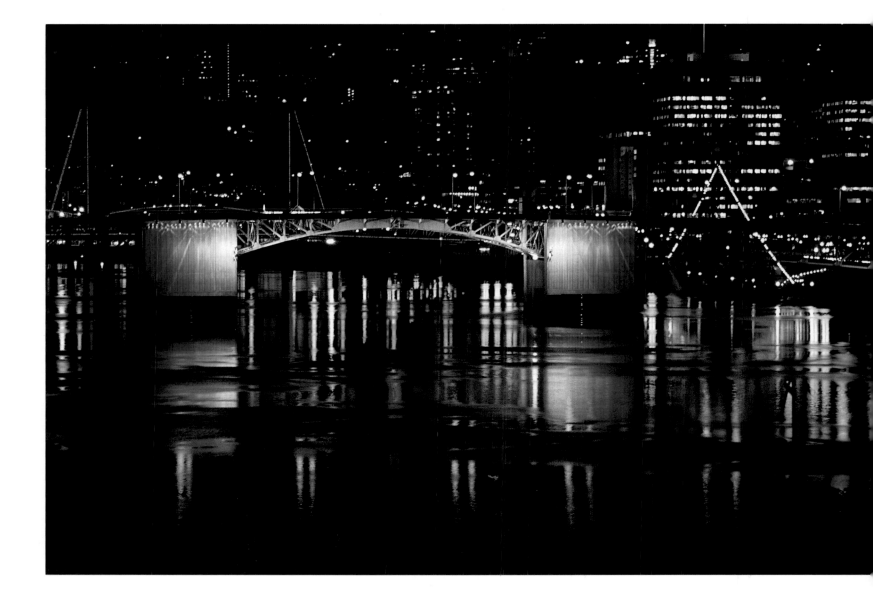

Architect Bob Frasca initially designed the soaring twin towers to suspend the roof of the Oregon Convention Center. But by the time the engineering concept changed and the towers lost their function, both Frasca and the public had become so fond of the idea that the glass towers were retained. Technically, they serve as skylights. And figuratively, they serve as hood ornaments, making key visual connections between the east and west banks of the river. ◄ An organization dubbed the Willamette Light Brigade led the charge to illuminate the bridges of the city. Half a league, half a league, half a league onward they rode—first triumphing over the Morrison Bridge. ▲

Much of Portland's charm and intimacy is a product of its small 200-foot-square downtown blocks. But city founders Asa Lovejoy and Francis Pettygrove were not thinking of intimacy and charm. They laid out each block, including half the adjoining streets, to cover one acre—just enough for a home, a garden, and one grazing cow. ▲ Portlanders love to tell tales about how mild the winters are out here—especially to relatives from the Midwest. Occasionally, however, January gives the city the cold shoulder, making the West Hills look a bit like Duluth. These Arctic blasts sometimes are followed by one of the most spectacular of Mother Nature's performances—a silver thaw. ▶

A light rain was falling as she came upriver, head held high in the wind, one hand reaching down to brush the swells that rolled to greet her. Thousands lined the river's banks to watch the progress of the barge that bore her. Thousands more thronged the bridges as she passed beneath the city's portals, heading for her place of honor in the center of their town. Finally, as she was hauled along downtown streets, the seamless crowd pressed forward. Parents raised high their children; tiny fingers stretched to touch the huge, outstretched hand.

They knew that Portlandia was the largest hammered copper sculpture to be commissioned since the Statue of Liberty, that she was a six-ton present to Portland, a gift to the citizens from themselves. But what spurred them this October dawn to spontaneous celebration was that the statue was a symbol of their city—young, alive, questing. And they wanted to make sure this, her first day in town, would be long remembered.

There are bigger ones, brasher ones, slicker ones, and showier ones, many fancier by far. But there is not anywhere a city of which its residents feel more fond.

Livability. The word so often used to describe Portland's key characteristic is a thoroughly contemporary one. But it refers to a distinctly old-fashioned notion. Portlanders say their city just *feels* right.

Nobody has ever described Portland as a metropolis. The city is compact, manageable, human-scaled. Even toward the tail end of the twentieth century, the average citizen commutes for fewer than thirty minutes to work, walks two blocks each day for lunch, and is home in plenty of time to pull a few weeds from the rose garden before dinner.

If that all sounds too contrived, too cozy, too comfy, too—well, let's just say it—too provincial, Portlanders simply shrug. They rejoice each time potential émigrés decline to flee the peril of big city life for paradise on the frontier.

Portland has its architectural pantheon, its Beaux-Art matrons in their terra-cotta finery, its cast-iron dowagers so primly pilastered, its art-deco flappers, its postmodern Madonna—a little heavier on hype than substance. All of this is preserved and protected, scrubbed by rain and polished by pride into what has been hailed as a carefully curated museum of frozen music. But despite the oft-heard hosannas of the architectural critics, Portland is not a city to be looked at. It's a city to be lived in.

———

Portland is thousands of runners ribboning through downtown streets during the Cascade Run-Off. It's office workers lingering late after lunchhour performances in Pioneer Courthouse Square. It's families crowding evening concerts in Waterfront Park.

It's fans packing the basketball arena, even when the Blazers are playing the worst team in the NBA. Browsers thronging bookstores and art galleries. Petitioners seeking signatures for a ballot measure.

It's liberals lining up Volvos at the recycling center. It's counting the advent of natural ale atop the list of recent civic improvements.

It's dawn on the river, a solitary scull floating in and out of the fog. It's noon in Northwest Portland, a couple scurrying to what surely must be the world's teeniest restaurant, a solitary table for two. It's late night, the party faithful gathering for final sets in a hundred haunts of jazz.

It's students at Reed College, maintaining the school's radical traditions by strolling, naked as jaybirds, through the immaculately groomed croquet players gathered on the college lawn.

It's the hustle of Chinatown, the bustle of Burnside, the madcap miscellany of Hawthorne, the stately promenade along RiverPlace.

It's fishermen landing steelhead in the shadow of downtown towers. It's kids splashing in the Salmon Street Springs. It's cops, on bikes and horses, stopping to chat with every child.

Portland is four hundred thousand people who line the streets in a June drizzle for the Rose Festival's Grand Floral Parade. Portland is people who actually talk to each other in an elevator.

It's houseboats and great blue herons, horse carriage rides and bicycle rickshaws. It's shooting hoops out in the street and picking blackberries by the wayside. It's lovers strolling through the evening light.

It's a neon sign of a stag whose nose turns red each Christmas. Portland is going to the Saturday Market on Sunday. Portland is rain that doesn't get you wet.

So popular is Portlandia that her guardian, the Metropolitan Arts Commission, receives endless requests for her to come out and play. One group even wanted to sell chocolate Portlandias. ◄ *Portlandia receives a warm, wet welcome.* ▼

Downtown, it's a drinking fountain on every corner lest loggers thirst for something likely to make them late getting back to the woods.

It's a cowboy sipping bourbon in a bar called Brasserie Montmartre. It's croissants at the rodeo. It's a birthday party for an elephant and dinner at Jake's. It's places called Macheesmo Mouse and Rimsky-Korsakoffee House. It's a Langlitz leather jacket. It's *The Oregonian* every morning. It's waiting in line for the sale at the Nike Factory Outlet store. It's a picnic in the park.

It's a toe dipped in the fountain between acts at the Civic Auditorium. It's skiers sneaking out from work early for an evening on the mountain. It's a wedding in the Rose Gardens. And it's softball on a Saturday in the summer in the rain.

And finally—and often—it's muted days of clement cloud, good friends around the fire.

———

Nowhere are these fruits of Portland life more obvious than in its rich quilt of neighborhoods. From its earliest days, Portland has described itself as the "City of Homes and Gardens." Apartment living did not much develop here until the 1950s. Apartment dwellers and their even more contemporary cousins—condomaniacs—still are regarded with a degree of suspicion by most Portlanders, for whom the backyard barbecue—especially the backyard barbecue conducted in a light summer rainstorm—is a sacred rite.

In Portland, recipes for special sauces to pour over freshly seared salmon are closely guarded family secrets.

The city divides into distinct neighborhoods of single-family homes, each with its unique tenor and community flavor. There are vista-rich retreats along the Alameda Ridge, manicured mansions in Dunthorpe, blue-collar bungalows in St. Johns, antique-stuffed storefronts strewn along the streets of Sellwood, cheek-by-jowl Victorians in Northwest Portland, and stately homes on Portland Heights. Each Portlander feels intensely loyal to his or her own neighborhood, proud of everything from its school to its ice cream shop, its *joie de vivre* to its jogging trail.

Who, then, is this Portlander, this creature so keen to get involved in everything, so ready to stand up and be counted, so religious about all civic duties except church-going, so passionate about recycling and rhododendrons?

He may wear a tie, but the collar is likely to be loosened at the neck. She may sport a silk dress, but her sneakers are in her purse.

Quirky, yes. Stubborn, certainly. Maverick, to a fault.

But also careful, conservative, controlled.

These twin traits—odd bedfellows indeed—are intertwined throughout the city's history. And not always in harmony. They survive as key characteristics because, though no modernist would admit it, Portland is a city firmly rooted in its past.

The place was founded by the quintessential odd couple—a civil servant and a drifter.

It was one fall morning in 1843 when Asa Lovejoy, who had just come West by wagon, and William Overton, remembered solely as "a rollicking fellow" who drifted in with the tide, took a canoe trip from the pioneer outpost of Fort Vancouver upstream to Oregon City. En route, they stopped near the great bend in the river, at a place the Indians had cleared by collecting firewood. As Overton stepped from the boat, there before him, soaring above the oaks and cottonwood, were the fir-studded hills. Across the river stretched the flatland, its gentle ripples broken only by volcanic buttes. And all this was set against the magnificent backdrop of the ever-glistening Cascades.

It must have been one of those days, generally every third, when the Cascades are visible.

Overton immediately was struck both by the potential and by his pecuniary predicament. He was broke. With Lovejoy he promptly struck a deal. For the twenty-five-cent filing fee, the rock-solid New Englander could have half the "rollicking fellow's" claim. Thus was the city of Portland founded—on a whim and a loan.

Overton laid plans for a tomahawk claim—marking the boundaries of a 640-acre township by blazing the trunks of trees. But he didn't stick around long enough to develop his idea. After a few months of felling trees and selling off shingles, Overton drifted off, fading from the pages of history.

Lovejoy was joined by a new partner, Francis Pettygrove, who picked up Overton's half of the claim. Thus was set the stage for the celebrated coin toss and the emergence of the city that was almost Boston.

No plans of any self-respecting Portland golfer would ever be thwarted by a shower of rain. ▼ *Azaleas get their moment of glory, holding their own amid the heady competition of Portland's International Rhododendron Test Garden.* ►

Each man was determined to name the new township after his hometown. Pettygrove, from Portland, Maine, won on two tosses out of three.

As a pioneer city, Portland was founded on the notion of absorbing only the best of what the rest of the world had to offer, and then remaining resolute in charting its own course. Portland always has been, above all else, determined to go its own way.

The town that emerged during the 1850s was an anomaly—prim white planks set stubborn against a backdrop of forest green, New England-proper with bear and cougar at the edge of town.

In a manner not always metaphorical, there still are bear and cougar at the edge of town. The inclusion within Portland's city limits of Forest Park—claimed to be the largest urban park in the nation—keeps creatures great and small close to the city's core. But in Portland, big isn't always better. The city also boasts the smallest park in the world, Mill Ends Park, the twenty-four-inch diameter site of a displaced power pole.

The early development of the new township hinged on its position on the Willamette as a deep-water port, and on the driving of Canyon Road through from the riverfront to the fertile agricultural region of the Tualatin Valley. Once farmers could get their produce to the waterfront, and once the California Gold Rush created a huge market for the bounty of Oregon, Portland's development as a trading city was assured.

Growth proceeded steadily until the 1905 fair commemorating the centenary of the Lewis and Clark Expedition sent the Portland story singing from coast to coast. The secret was out. Five years later, the city's population had jumped from one hundred thousand to a quarter of a million. This growth prompted a tidal wave of building in the heart of the city, producing those distinctive classical revival monuments that still provide the signature of downtown.

Following this heady bout of boosterism, the city hurriedly returned to its beloved low profile. For decades, travelers helter-skeltering between San Francisco and Seattle zipped right past. And Portlanders were delighted. Not until the out-break of World War II, when Henry Kaiser's shipyards began turning out so many ships that a call went out for seventy thousand new workers, did the city begin once more to boom.

Today the port remains a key player in the local economy, as a major center for exporting wheat and wood products, for importing cars and minerals. Employment remains high in lumber products, metalworking, sportswear, publishing, and food products. And a cadre of high-tech entrepreneurs takes root in Oregon's flourishing Silicon Forest. But Portland's primary economic strength lies now in being a regional center for service industries and retail trade, government and finance.

Poised on the Pacific Rim, pressing toward the crest of what it confidently predicts will be the century of the Pacific, Portland has one side of its personality restlessly roaming tomorrow's world. But the other remains close to home, where it always has been, content to bask in the bounty of Oregon and bother itself only with those smart enough to slow down and join in.

———

If the city occasionally seems too smug—and it does—it's because Portlanders sincerely believe they do a number of things better than anyone else. Foremost among those things is looking before it leaps.

Folks still bemoan the moment in 1871 when an inattentive citizenry allowed eight of the string of Park Blocks that had been set aside as a long promenade through the city's center to fall into private hands. And they are determined never to make such a mistake again. Portlanders take great pride in the effort in the 1970s that turned around the decline of the downtown core, and made it once more into a vibrant center, a place that refuses to fall silent at five.

Locals delight in telling visitors the tale of the highway that once roared along the west side of the Willamette River, how it was torn up to be replaced by the popular park that serves as the city's front yard. If Tom McCall Waterfront Park—named for the governor whose environmental passion led to cleaning up the river that had been allowed to become the city's sewer—is Portland's front lawn, then the city's living room is Pioneer Courthouse Square.

On this block, at the heart of the city, once stood its finest building, the Portland Hotel. In 1950, the seven-story chateau was razed. In the name of progress, the block became a parking lot. In the name of livability, citizens clamored to

Laurelhurst Park is a place for picnics, for tossing horseshoes, but not for feeding the ducks. It is also perfect for finding a quiet moment to gaze at an old oak tree. ◄ *The Chiles Center hugs the bluff at the University of Portland.* ▼

turn it into a public square. Their efforts long were thwarted by private and political power. Eventually, citizens took matters into their own hands. More than sixty-five thousand of them ponied up fifteen dollars each for a brick bearing a name—and the public square was paved.

Further efforts to enhance the quality of downtown life have included building residential units near the city center, insisting that all high-rise towers boast people-friendly retail spaces on their ground floors, and creating a light-rail mass transit system hailed as one of the nation's finest.

This recent effort to keep the gridlock wolf from the door has provided Portlanders with their latest opportunity to lord it over their arch rivals in Seattle, a city where rush hour lasts all day.

And finally, after 150 years of pretending not to notice as the river formed a boundary between Portland's power structure on the west side and its growing population on the east side, a carefully choreographed plan seeks to bring the east bank into full partnership in the city's commercial life. Here rise a revamped shopping mall and a new Convention Center with its trademark twin glass towers. Here stand no fewer than seventy inner-city blocks earmarked at last for integration into the city's heart.

———

One other feature of Portland must be noted— the ease with which its citizens can flee the city. Founded as an Eden carved from wilderness, the city remains strikingly close to unspoiled places. Located within a hundred-mile radius of video game arcades and stores selling fax machines is an unmatched array of natural wonders.

To the west wait ocean beaches, washed by wind and rain squalls, small towns brimming with saltwater taffy and starfish, kite flyers and clam chowder.

To the south lies the Willamette Valley, dotted with fruit trees and vineyards, postcard-perfect barns and covered bridges, its soil so fecund fenceposts seem to send up shoots each spring.

To the east snakes the Columbia Gorge, the gateway to the high desert country of spur and saddle, of sage and endless sky.

And always on the horizon soar the sentinels of our sky, the snow-capped volcanic peaks—one alive and one dormant—reminders of Mother Nature's power at our door.

Above all else, Portland is a city of oddballs, of characters, of people who like to feel passionate about where they live. Some are homegrown. Others have come from all across the world, drawn to share in this very special experiment of taking care of a very special corner of our planet. Portlanders to this day delight in telling the surely apocryphal tale of the branch in the Oregon Trail. The route south, to California, allegedly was marked by a piece of gold. To the north pointed a sign: "To Portland."

People who could read came here.

Reading—followed by thinking and talking about what it has read and learned—remains one of the town's favorite pastimes.

Portland's pride is nowhere better evidenced than in its 213 bookstores. Still, the grandest of them all, Powell's, never is hailed as the world's biggest. Portlanders leave such claims to Texans. "Powell's?" they say. "The biggest bookstore in the world? I've no idea. But I do know it's the best."

Proud, then, and passionate. But most of all involved. No Portlander is permitted to forget the city's unofficial motto, the inscription carved on the Skidmore Fountain: "Good Citizens Are the Riches of a City."

Collectively, Portlanders are individualists— people fully prepared to listen to others, but mostly, and resolutely, determined to go their own way. That passion for doing their own thing has led to one of the biggest misconceptions about Portlanders—the notion that they do not really like visitors. It was Oregon's Governor Tom McCall who once said, "Come visit, but please don't stay."

Everyone remembers that part of the quote. Forgotten has been the rest of Tom's sentence: "Come visit, but please don't stay unless you are prepared to play by our rules."

Thanks to Portland's rules, it is a place of clean air and clean rivers and clean streets, a place determined to avoid the sprawl and attendant social evils that have consumed so many cities. Portland is a place where people are determined to take care of each other and their environment. It's a place that takes very seriously its notion of livability, and works very hard to make sure that it shows.

This is what makes people want to come here. This is what makes them want to stay.

The Visitors Association and the World Trade Center sing Portland's song. ▼
Ten bridges span the Willamette River. ▶ *"Portland is the biggest downtown success story in America," said Don Canty, editor of* Architecture *magazine.* ▶▶

Its the ideal that was first crafted by Greek philosophers and town planners—every project has a responsibility to the past and to the future. Forging those links is what Portland architects did best in the 1980s. And in the process, they created a city that is inviting and friendly, where new buildings stand as good neighbors to the old. ◄ Albers Mill, home of Oregon's Wheat Marketing Center, is one of the historic structures finding a new lease on life on the north downtown waterfront. ▲

Flower sellers blossom downtown in springtime. ▲ Which windows really open? This example of *tromp l'oeil*—a trick of the eye—on a wall of the Oregon Historical Society provides Portlanders with one of their favorite pastimes—asking visitors to decide which window is real. Illusionism in painting murals on buildings first was practiced in ancient Greece. ▶

Form follows function. Because of its height and exposure to the wind, the Fremont Bridge, which opened in 1973, is equipped with the sort of ice detectors used at major airports. As hazardous conditions develop on the bridge, data is transmitted by microwave to ever-attentive road crews. ◄   Hand in hand, old and new coexist at the foot of Security Pacific Plaza. ▲

RiverPlace brought to Portland a downtown marina, a waterfront hotel, and a flourishing community of riverbank condominiums—all of which seemed terribly modern at the time. But RiverPlace also has provided Portland citizens with a location for the revival of a distinctly old-fashioned tradition—the summer evening promenade. ▲ Portland's rivers always have played a key role in the city's commercial life, furnishing a vital link between the productive agricultural hinterland and the opportunity of trade across the high seas. But they also long have played another role—as wonderful places to have fun. ▶

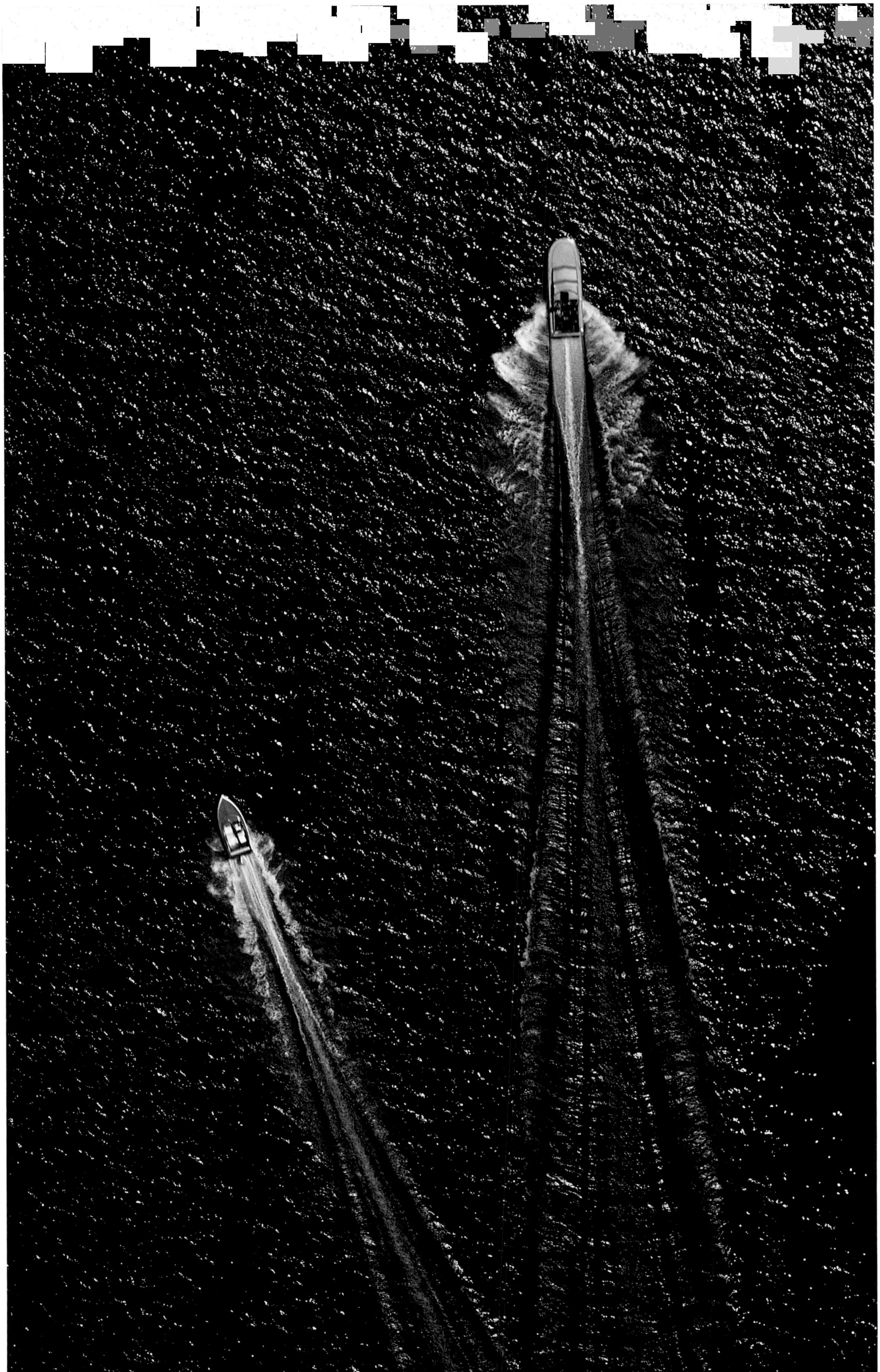

Most cities have fountains. And in many places, stern-faced police officers steadfastly arrest any and all folks who dare set foot in their waters. Portland takes a different approach, encouraging people to get all wet. By day, Forecourt Fountain, overlooked by the First Interstate Tower, resounds with squeals of children. By night, it becomes the focal point for concertgoers, who step out between acts at Civic Auditorium to cool off. ◄   Part crime-fighting patrol and part public relations coup, the Police Mounted Patrol is a favorite sight on downtown streets. ▲

Downtowns that thrive are the ones that refuse to turn off the lights when office workers call it a day. Faced in the 1970s and 1980s with rising competition from suburban shopping malls, Portland's downtown launched a coordinated private and public effort to preserve its status as a major retailing center. That effort was capped in 1990 by the opening of Pioneer Place. ▲ Bilingual street names point the way in historic Chinatown. ▶

Man cannot live by bread and beer alone. But it's a pretty good start. A renaissance in the art of boutique baking sends the aromatic promise of dough on the rise wafting along downtown sidewalks. ◄ The Elephant & Castle is one of scores of pubs and restaurants selling the fruit of Portland's burgeoning crop of microbreweries—each producing fresh and natural ales. ▲ Sunday in the park with George. Alice and Mom came, too. ►►

An island of calm in the storm-tossed sea of city life, the Vietnam Veterans Memorial identifies 751 Oregonians killed in action. Names are etched on black granite. One panel bears no names. ▲ Designed to highlight Zen principles of simplicity and harmony, Portland's Japanese Gardens revive and restore. ▶

Their "living room." That's how Portlanders refer to the delightfully eclectic public square they created from an eyesore—the surface parking lot sitting in the heart of downtown. Here, people may wander slowly, heads bowed, but they are not deep in meditation. They are searching for their names, etched in the bricks that pave the square. ◄ Crowds throng Pioneer Courthouse Square for everything from chamber music recitals to political rallies, rock concerts to the annual Festival of Flowers. ▲

Our first streetcar was drawn by a mule, reminding us that Portlanders long have fought the battle to fend off the automobile. MAX—the Metropolitan Area Express—has been hailed as the country's finest mass transit light-rail system. ▲ Portlanders were so fond of playing in their fountains that designers crafted one just for fun. Children delight in scampering through the ever-changing patterns of Salmon Street Springs. And by night, lovers take a break from gazing into each other's eyes. ►

One child plus one playground equals happiness. ◄ Noah may have run a pretty good ark, but he wouldn't have made much of a zookeeper. The world's best zoos don't do a little bit of everything. Washington Park Zoo, for example, chooses to specialize in doing a handful of things well. This has resulted in its status as the world leader in breeding Asian elephants. ▲

Downtown is not just a place to visit. It's a place to call home. This is another key piece set in the jigsaw of inner-city livability. More and more Portlanders are opting for the considerable joy of walking to work. These apartments overlook the South Park Blocks. ▲ Kids hurry along to school in North Portland. ▶

Tom McCall Waterfront Park,
Portland's front lawn, is home to a seemingly endless series
of summer festivals featuring music—rock, classical, country,
blues, and jazz—by local favorites such as the Tom Grant Band.
It's also a hot spot for riverfront strolling, lunchtime jogging,
and watching the endless parade of activity upon the river. ◄
Victorian painted ladies show off their latest makeovers on the
streets of Northwest Portland. ▲

In some cities, a man's home is his castle. In Portland, a couple's castle is their backyard. ▲ Rain or shine, summer or winter, hoopsters turn their backs on gymnasiums to shoot baskets in the park. ► Portland is where the mayor bicycles to work. The city, criss-crossed by a network of bicycle paths and trails, serves as home base for the annual Cycle Oregon tour. Each fall, this event attracts thousands of cyclists from all across the country for a week-long ride through the backroads of Oregon. ►►

One NBA coach complained that playing in Portland's Memorial Coliseum was like playing to a theater crowd. Portlanders took it as a compliment. ◄ At Portland International Raceway, Rick Mears locks fear from his eyes as he prepares for one of the Rose Festival's most colorful attractions—Indy car racing. ▲

On a gray Sunday morning in March, there are other things a guy could do. He could hang around the house, fixing that leaking faucet. Or paint the kitchen ceiling. Or even change the oil in the car. But some mornings the only thing that makes sense is to take the truck and the wife out to Sauvie Island and watch the clouds roll by. ▲ Happiness is the Columbia River, a steady wind in your sails, a familiar face on the horizon. ▶

It surely would be foolhardy in football, and downright dangerous in boxing. But once each year fans of one Portland sport get to suit up and test their skills against the pros. The Cascade Run-Off draws to town the world's finest fifteen-kilometer runners. Locals delight in taking them on. ◄   Cleaning up the Willamette has brought salmon and steelhead back within reach of poles cast in the cool shadows of the city's bridges. ▲

Fireworks fill the night sky over the city. ▲ Get it out of the galleries and onto the streets. Portlanders leap at any excuse to turn out by the thousands and drive traffic from their downtown streets. Artquake, the annual celebration that lures the arts into the open air, provides a perfect opportunity. ►

Each June, some four hundred thousand people line downtown streets for the Rose Festival's Grand Floral Parade. Hundreds of hands help affix flowers to the floats. ◄ A few final adjustments to the uniforms, a last-minute licking of the lips, and on with the parade. ▲ Dragon dancers crash through Chinatown. ►►

In 1835, someone showed up at the Salem wedding of Jason Lee and Anna Marian Pittman with an unusual gift—the first rosebush to reach Oregon—arriving by way of Cape Horn. Cuttings from that bush later flourished in Portland, giving the city its emblem. During the Rose Festival, which has been celebrated each year since 1907, Navy ships tie up at the harbor wall. ▲ Crewed by raucous paddlers, dragon boats sprint to snatch the flag. ▶

A bench beneath the elms that line the South Park Blocks provides the perfect rehearsal hall for a couple of Portland State University students. ▲ Summer evenings turn the waterfront into a prime people-watching place. ► Maestro James DePreist leads the Oregon Symphony Orchestra in its rehearsal. ►►

Poetry in motion. It begins with a gaggle of seven-year-olds showing up for Saturday morning class. But for most of these tots, the years of training will prove tutu tough. Only a handful will make it to the spotlight with the Oregon Ballet. ◄ Students from all across the city are attracted by magnet programs at Jefferson High that offer the chance to study with professional resident artists in courses of dance, music, and theater. ▲

The Portland Opera kicks up its skirts. ▲ When Soviet classical pianist Andrei Kitaev fled Moscow in search of an opportunity to play the music he loved—jazz—he came to what he called America's richest live jazz city. "Portland," he said, "is the place where I can play with great musicians four or five nights a week—for people who will come not to eat, but to listen." Here, Sonny Rollins wails at the Mount Hood Festival of Jazz. ▶

Putting on the Schnitz. Once abandoned to ghosts and cobwebs, to fading acts and broken seats, a downtown concert hall received a major rejuvenation to emerge as the Arlene Schnitzer Concert Hall—affectionately dubbed "The Schnitz." ◄   In the 1870s, many cities banned croquet. Ladies were in the habit of revealing their ankles when taking spirited swings with their mallets. Sex appeal remains a key component amid the hushed tones and polite applause that surround the competition at the annual tournament on the greensward at Reed College. ▲

A Hollywood film crew roams in search of realism and finds that an Old Town street readily converts to a 1940s movie set. ▲ Pottery. Paintings. Jewelry. Wood carvings. Leatherwork. Trinkets and tidbits. Baubles and beads. And a sinfully sweet delicacy dubbed the *elephant ear.* Portland's home of handcrafted items is the Saturday Market. And it's open on Sunday, too. ▶

Keep on forklift trucking. ◄
A construction worker finds rainbow suspenders brighten a
long day of jousting with joists. ▲ Looking like beads on an
Indian blanket, thousands of new cars line the quayside at the
Port of Portland. Automobiles from Japan are one of Portland's
major imports. From here they are transported by rail to dealers
all over the United States. ►►

When grain was first shipped from Portland to London in the 1860s, the English refused it. Brokers were convinced any wheat that plump must be waterlogged. No such problems plague the industry today as the world recognizes the region's reputation for grain bulging at the seams. ▲ Tools of the trade in Oregon's Silicon Forest bear no resemblance to chainsaws. ▶

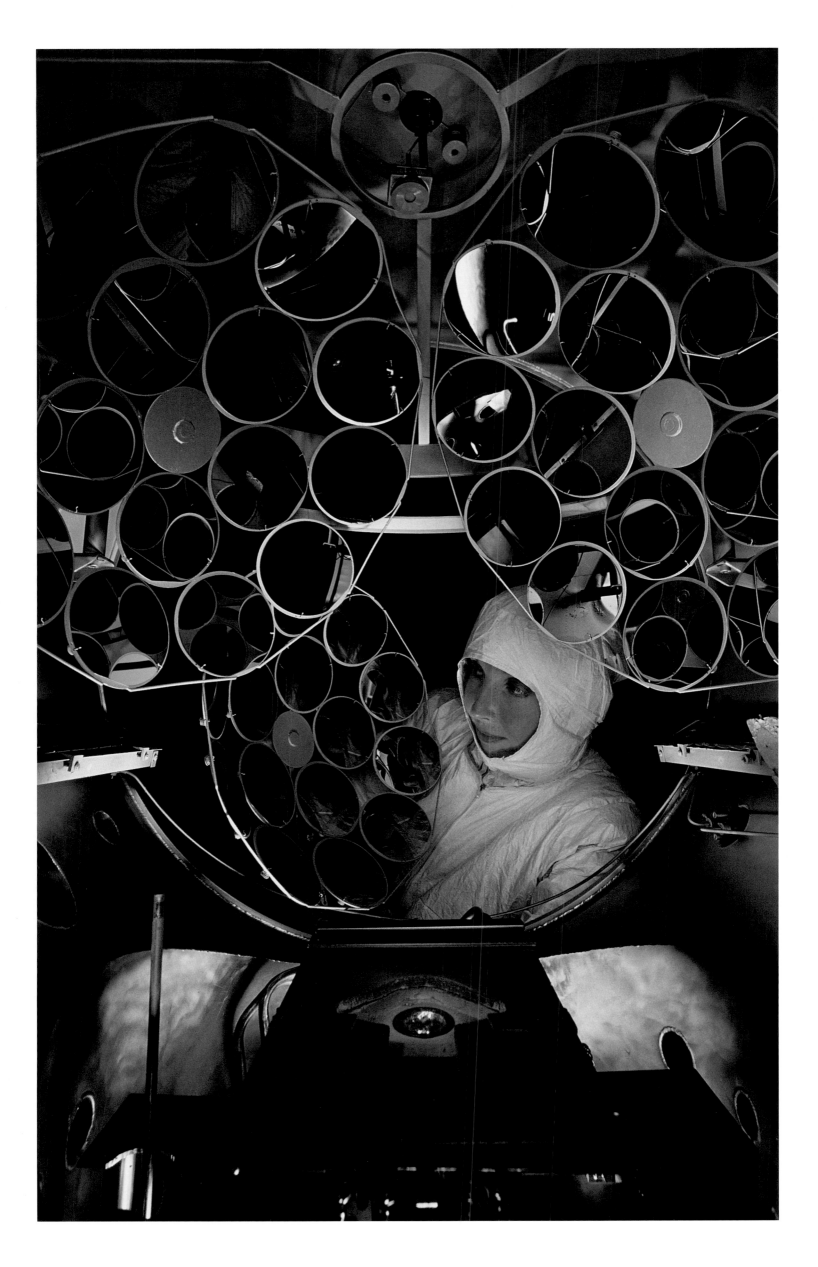

It may not be the Eiffel Tower. But it does catch the eye. The first question always is the same. How tall *is* that thing? The KGON Tower is 603 feet. That's 57 feet taller than the First Interstate Tower, which is 10 feet taller than Big Pink. ▶ "Green gold" loggers called it when first they saw the bounty of the Oregon forest. More recent residents recognize that trees have value standing in an ancient forest as well as slicing through a mill. ▲

Whether they are flying in from Bali or Bora Bora, Tacoma or Timbuktu, even the most jaded travelers press their noses to the windows as planes bank for the final approach to Portland International Airport. Newcomers are lost for words as the face of Mount Hood looms into view. But Portlanders know exactly what to say. "Ah, home!" ▲ With nary a peep from Led Zeppelin, the sound of heavy metal roars through Oregon Steel Mills. ▶

It's a mystery, as unfathomable as it is intriguing. What primordial urge pulls salmon, after years of swimming in the ocean, back to the precise freshwater places of their birth? But there is no mystery to what is waiting for them as they near the end of their odyssey—a Willamette Falls welcoming committee armed with rod and reel. ◄ Most ports have huge cranes looming large in the background. The Port of Portland has Mount Hood. ▲

Rush hour on the river. And gridlock threatens the channel. ▲ They are Davids to the Goliaths of the ocean. Tiny tugboats pugnaciously push to and fro through the port, harnessing huge vessels to their will. Slowly but surely, brawn gives way to the bidding of the little engines that could. ▶

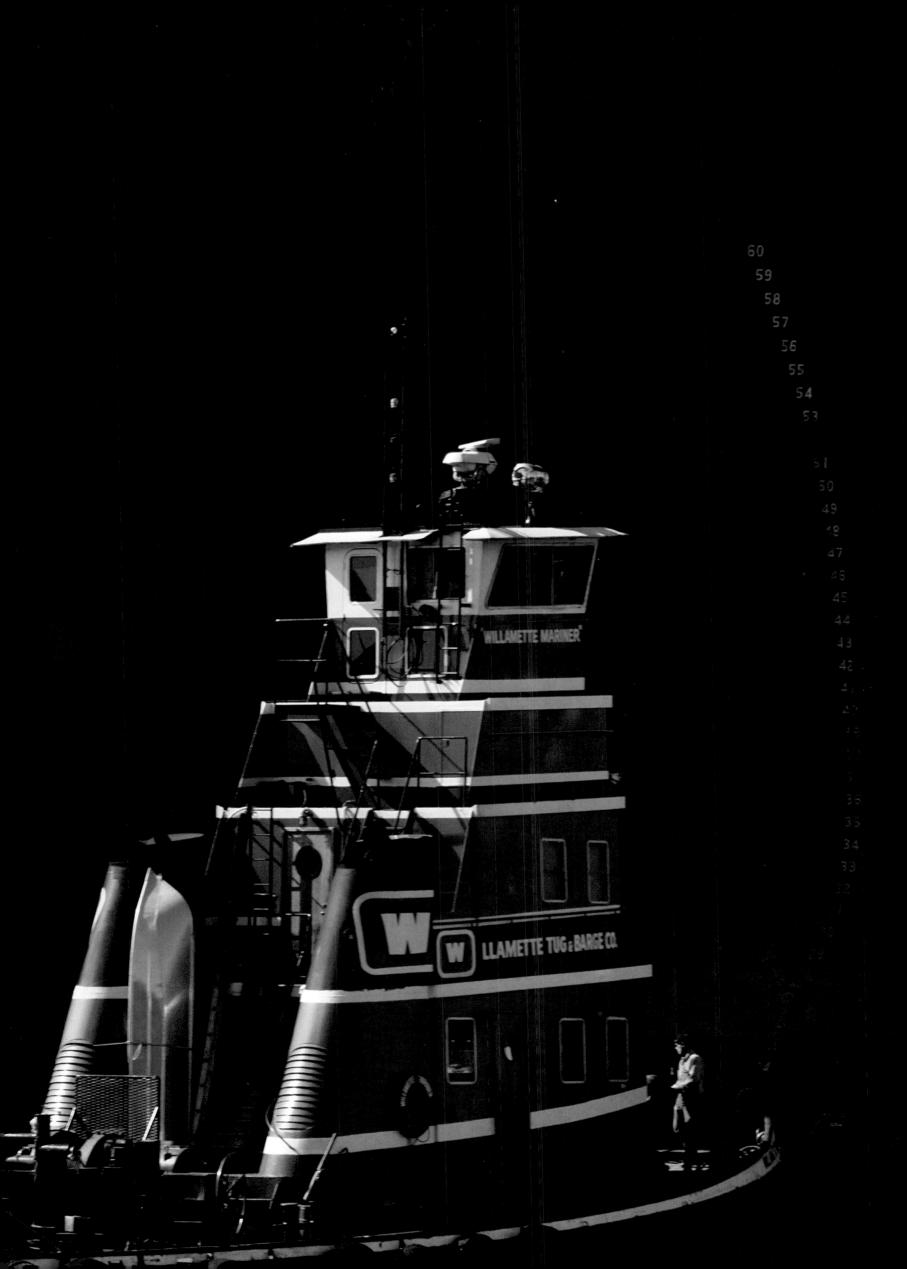

The earliest inhabitants of this region took to the water in cedar canoes, their paddles seeking dominion over eddy and tide. Contemporary craft may be a little sleeker, but the challenges—and the rewards—have remained the same. A solitary scull can slip from the downtown marina at dawn, and in moments the oarsman loses himself in the seamless flow of memory and current. ◄ The Fremont Bridge basks in evening light. ▲

There may be the *occasional* day in Oregon when it seems more sensible to bring a windbreaker than a bathing suit to the beach. Still, the intrepid visitor does not worry. He simply takes that time-honored advice: go fly a kite. ▲ The Columbia Gorge has exactly two things going for it as one of the world's hottest places for boardsailing—a wind blowing one way and a current flowing the other. ► Some Oregon spots speak for themselves. Take Crown Point, for example. ►►

Settlers were drawn West by tales of a garden of Eden at the end of the Oregon Trail. History failed to record whether they were told it was a flower garden. ◄ Vineyards are newcomers to the hills around the Valley. Locals, sipping the bounty of the pinot noir harvest, ask why nobody ever thought of this before. ▲

One man, one rod, and one mountain. The only thing tricky about catching fish in Trillium Lake is watching what you're doing rather than watching the play of light upon the mountain. ▲ After weeks of worrying, days of waiting, and hours of wondering how it will feel, finally it all comes down to this. The cowboy has a few moments to ready himself before the bull bursts from the chute. Win or lose, the contest will be over in eight seconds. Then it will be time to start worrying again. ▶

All that glitters is not gold. But the KOIN Tower does a pretty good impersonation of bullion as it basks in the setting sun. ◄   Of all the character traits of the average Portlander, none is more significant than this. He is someone who believes problems can be solved, that when things go wrong—by joining hands with others, by pitching in with work and time and effort—things can be put right. That's a nice notion on which citizens can dwell each day as dusk settles upon their city. ▲